M000158878

Francesca Moody Productions

FEELING AFRAID AS IF SOMETHING TERRIBLE IS GOING TO HAPPEN

by Marcelo Dos Santos

Feeling Afraid As If Something Terrible Is Going To Happen
premiered in ROUNDABOUT at Summerhall
as part of the Edinburgh Fringe Festival,
produced by Francesca Moody Productions.

FEELING AFRAID AS IF SOMETHING TERRIBLE IS GOING TO HAPPEN

by Marcelo Dos Santos

CREATIVE TEAM

Writer	Marcelo Dos Santos
Director	Matthew Xia
Lighting	Elliot Griggs
Sound	Max Pappenheim
Stage Manager	Chloë Forestier-Walker
Executive Producer	Francesca Moody
Producer	Harriet Bolwell
Production Manager	Ed Borgnis
Design Consultant	Kat Heath
Additional Dramaturgical Support	Oscar Toeman
PR	SM Publicity

CAST

THE COMEDIAN	Samuel Barnett

Special thanks to Ariel Levy, DMLK, Giles Moody, Julie Clare, Michael Windsor Ungureanu, Paines Plough, Richard Lakos, Riverside Studios, Simon Blakey, Matthew Littleford and Theadora Alexander.

This production has been licensed by arrangement with The Agency (London) Ltd, 24 Pottery Lane, London W11 4LZ, email: info@theagency.co.uk

CREATIVE TEAM

MARCELO DOS SANTOS | WRITER
Marcelo is an award-winning British/Brazilian/Australian playwright and screenwriter. In 2014 he adapted the critically acclaimed *Lionboy* for Complicité, which toured extensively in the UK and internationally including to the New Victory Theater on Broadway.

He is currently under commission to the Michael Grandage Company and the English Touring Theatre (ETT).

Other credits include: *Subverts* (Living Newspaper, Edition 5, Royal Court Theatre); *Trigger Warning* (Camden People's Theatre, co-created with Natasha Nixon); *New Labour* (RADA, directed by Richard Wilson); *The End of History* (High Hearted Theatre/Soho Theatre); *Open Plan* (Royal Welsh College of Music & Drama); *Cheer Up This Is Only The Beginning* (co-writer Liverpool Everyman and Playhouse); *Moshing Lying Down* (Shunt Vaults); *Lovers Walk* (Southwark Playhouse).

He has been a writer on attachment at the Bush Theatre, HighTide Festival Theatre and the Royal Court Theatre. He was also a member of the BBC Drama Room 2019/20.

SAMUEL BARNETT | THE COMEDIAN
Samuel Barnett is a two-time Tony nominee, for the Broadway productions of *The History Boys* and *Twelfth Night*, respectively. Samuel played the title role in *Dirk Gently's Detective Agency* for BBC America. He most recently starred in *Straight Line Crazy* opposite Ralph Fiennes at the Bridge Theatre, written by David Hare and directed by Nicholas Hytner.

His other theatre credits include: *Allelujah!* for the Bridge Theatre, *Kiss of the Spiderwoman* and *Dealer's Choice* for the Menier Chocolate Factory, *An Oak Tree*, *The Beaux Stratagem* and *Women Beware Women* for the National Theatre, *Richard III* and *Twelfth Night* for The Globe Theatre and Broadway, *The Way of the World* for Sheffield Theatres, *Rosencrantz and Guildenstern are Dead* and *The Accrington Pals* for Chichester Festival Theatre, *The Marriage of Figaro* for Manchester Royal Exchange, *The Man* at The Finborough Theatre, *When You Cure Me* and *The Whisky Taster* at The Bush Theatre.

His television credits include: *Four Lives*, *The Amazing Mr Blunden*, *The Prince*, *Penny Dreadful*, *Endeavour*, *Not Safe For Work*, *Twenty Twelve*, *Beautiful People*, *Desperate Romantics*, *John Adams*, *Vicious*, *Strange*, *Murder in Provence*.

His film credits include: *The Lady in the Van*, *The History Boys*, *Jupiter Ascending*, *Bright Star* and *Mrs Henderson Presents*.

MATTHEW XIA | DIRECTOR

Matthew Xia is the Artistic Director of ATC (Actors Touring Company). He was previously Associate Artistic Director at the Royal Exchange Theatre (where he established the OPEN EXCHANGE, an artist development scheme for over 400 next generation theatre-makers), Director in Residence at The Liverpool Everyman & Playhouse and Associate Director at Theatre Royal Stratford East.

Directing credits include: *The Wiz* (Ameena Hamid Productions/Hope Mill/ Chuchu Nwagu); *Rice* (ATC/Orange Tree); *Family Tree* (Greenwich & Docklands International Festival/ATC); *846 Live* (Theatre Royal Stratford East/Greenwich & Docklands International Festival); *Amsterdam* (ATC/Orange Tree/Plymouth Theatre Royal); *Blood Knot* (Orange Tree); *Eden* (Hampstead Theatre); *One Night In Miami…* (Nottingham Playhouse/Bristol Old Vic/HOME); *Into The Woods*, *Frankenstein* (Royal Exchange Theatre); *Wish List* (Royal Exchange Theatre/Royal Court); *Shebeen* (Nottingham Playhouse/Theatre Royal Stratford East); *Sleeping Beauty* (Theatre Royal Stratford East); *Dublin Carol* (Sherman Theatre); *Blue/Orange, The Sound of Yellow* (Young Vic); *Sizwe Banzi Is Dead* (Young Vic/ Eclipse); *Migration Music, Scrappers* (Liverpool Everyman & Playhouse); *Cinderella, The Blacks* (Co-Director, Theatre Royal Stratford East); *I Was Looking at the Ceiling and Then I Saw the Sky* (Co-Director, Theatre Royal Stratford East/The Barbican); *Suckerpunch Boom Suite* (The Barbican/ NitroBEAT); *Mad Blud*, *Aladdin* (Associate Director, Theatre Royal Stratford East).

Composing/Sound Design credits include: London Paralympics Opening Ceremony (DJ); *The People are Singing* (Royal Exchange); *Free Run* (Underbelly); *That's The Way To Do It* (TimeWontWait); *Pass The Baton, Bolero Remixed* (New London Orchestra); *Da Boyz, Family Man, The Snow Queen, Hansel & Gretel, Medea*, and *Squid* (Theatre Royal Stratford East).

Matthew is a founding member of Act for Change. In 2019, he was awarded an Honorary Doctorate from the University of the Arts London for his efforts to make theatre universally accessible by working to promote minority groups as theatre leaders, makers and consumers.

ELLIOT GRIGGS | LIGHTING DESIGNER

Elliot trained at RADA. Theatre work includes: *Amélie the Musical* (Criterion Theatre/The Other Palace/Watermill Theatre/UK tour. Nominated for Olivier Award for Best New Musical); *Fleabag* (Wyndham's Theatre/SoHo Playhouse, New York/Soho Theatre/Edinburgh Festival/tour. Nominated for Olivier Award for Best Entertainment or Comedy Play); *Purple Snowflakes and Titty Wanks, A Fight Against, On Bear Ridge* (Royal Court); *The Wild Duck* (Almeida); *The Lover/The Collection* (Harold Pinter Theatre); *An Octoroon* (Orange Tree/ National Theatre); *Jitney* (Old Vic/Leeds Playhouse/Headlong); *Missing Julie* (Theatre Clwyd); *Ivan and the Dogs* (Young Vic); *Richard III* (Headlong); *Disco Pigs* (Trafalgar Studios/Irish Rep, NY); *Dry Powder* (Hampstead Theatre); *Pomona* (Orange Tree Theatre/Royal Exchange/National Theatre. Off West End Award for Best Lighting Designer); *Queens of the Coal Age, The Night Watch* (Royal Exchange Theatre); *Missing People* (Leeds Playhouse/Kani Public Arts, Japan); *Yen* (Royal Court/Royal Exchange Theatre); *Blue Door* (Ustinov Studio); *Loot* (Park Theatre/Watermill Theatre); *Somnium* (Sadler's Wells); *The Misfortune of the English, Last Easter, The Sugar Syndrome, Low Level Panic, Sheppey, buckets* (Orange Tree); *Hir* (Bush Theatre); *Lampedusa* (HighTide); *The Oracles* (Punchdrunk); *Martha, Josie and the Chinese Elvis, Educating Rita* (Hull Truck); *Shift, Bromance* (Barely Methodical Troupe). Event and Exhibition Design includes: *100 Story Hotel* (Discover Story Centre); *Lost Lagoon, Height of Winter, The Single-Opticon, Alcoholic Architecture* (Bompas & Parr).

MAX PAPPENHEIM | SOUND DESIGNER

Recent theatre includes: *The Night of the Iguana, Cruise* (West End); *A Doll's House Part 2, Assembly, The Way of the World* (Donmar Warehouse); *The Children* (Royal Court/Broadway); *Ophelias Zimmer* (Schaubühne, Berlin/Royal Court); *The Fever Syndrome, Dry Powder, Sex with Strangers, Labyrinth* (Hampstead); *Old Bridge* (Bush Theatre. Off West End Award for Sound Design, Olivier Award for Outstanding Achievement in an Affiliate Theatre); *The Homecoming, My Cousin Rachel* (Theatre Royal Bath/national tour); *Crooked Dances* (Royal Shakespeare Company); *Kan Yama Kan* (Global Theatre, Riyadh); *Macbeth* (Chichester Festival Theatre); *One Night in Miami* (Nottingham Playhouse); *Hogarth's Progress* (Rose Theatre Kingston); *Waiting for Godot* (Sheffield Crucible); *The Ridiculous Darkness* (Gate Theatre); *Dragons and Mythical Beasts* (Regent's Park Open Air Theatre/national tour); *Amsterdam, Humble Boy, Blue/Heart, The Distance* (Orange Tree Theatre); *The Gaul* (Hull Truck); *Jane Wenham* (Out of Joint); *My Eyes Went Dark* (Traverse/ 59E59); *A Kettle of Fish* (Yard Theatre); *CommonWealth* (Almeida); *Creve Coeur* (Print Room); *Cuzco, Wink* (Theatre503); *Secret Life of Humans, Switzerland, Spamalot, The Glass Menagerie* (English Theatre of Frankfurt); *Yellowfin, Kiki's Delivery Service* (Southwark Playhouse); *Mrs Lowry and Son* (Trafalgar Studios); *Martine, Black Jesus, Somersaults* (Finborough); *A Splinter of Ice, Being Mr Wickham, The Habit of Art, Monogamy* (Original Theatre); *Looking Good Dead, Teddy, Toast, Fabric, Invincible* (National Tours). Online includes: *The System, Barnes' People, The Haunting of Alice Bowles* (Original Theatre); *15 Heroines* (Digital Theatre). Opera includes: *Miranda* (Opéra Comique, Paris); *Hansel and Gretel* (BYO/Opera Holland Park); *Bluebeard's Castle* (Theatre of Sound); *Scraww* (Trebah Gardens); *Vixen* (Vaults/international tour); *Carmen: Remastered* (ROH/Barbican). Radio includes: *Home Front* (BBC Radio 4). Associate Artist of The Faction and Silent Opera.

ED BORGNIS | PRODUCTION MANAGER

Ed is a Production Manager and Technical Director working in the UK and worldwide. Recent work includes: *Dogs of Europe* (Barbican/world touring for Belarus Free Theatre); *Jean Paul Gaultier's Fashion Freakshow* (world tour for RGM Productions); *Impossible* world tour (Jamie Hendry Productions); *Gay Times Honours* at Magazine London; *Black and Gold* (a Google Christmas Party at Camden Roundhouse); a series of *Star Wars* launch events for HP; and *The Grand Journey* (European tour for Bombay Sapphire). Ed has worked for the sound departments of the RSC, Royal Ballet, Regent's Park Open Air, The Globe, Kiln and various concert venues. He also dabbles in video design and provides broadcast engineering support for the BBC. Ed has a Postgraduate Engineering degree from University of Warwick and grew up in London and Norfolk.

CHLOË FORESTIER-WALKER | STAGE MANAGER

Stage management work includes: *Straight Line Crazy* (Bridge Theatre); *Platinum Jubilee, Pageant; Peggy For You, little scratch* (Hampstead Theatre); *Deciphering* (Curious Directive/New Diorama Theatre); *Arthur/Merlin* (Iris Theatre); *Kipps* (Mountview); *Dance:01, Freedom of Movement Festival* (Stanley Arts); *Everybody Cares, Everybody Understands* (Papercut Theatre/Vaults); *Sleeping Beauty* (The Leatherhead Theatre); *You Game* (RADA Studios Theatre); *The Niceties* (Finborough Theatre); *Frieda Loves Ya!* (Vaults, Edinburgh Fringe).

HARRIET BOLWELL | PRODUCER

Harriet is a theatre producer of new work. Recent credits include: *The Meaning of Zong* by Giles Terera ,*The Prick & The Sting* by Sharon Clark and *The Hatchling* by Trigger.

She has produced for Bristol Old Vic, Raucous, Trigger, Coney and Paines Plough, making all kinds of work in all kinds of places across the UK – from the highstreets of Plymouth to the Natural History Museum.

Previous Associate Producer credits with Francesca Moody Productions include *Baby Reindeer* by Richard Gadd, *Do Our Best* by Remy Beasley and *Square Go* by Gary McNair and Kieran Hurley. Harriet is also co-Director of Shedinburgh Fringe Festival.

Francesca Moody Productions commissions, develops and presents brave, entertaining and compelling new theatre. They work with the UK's leading playwrights and discover and nurture new talent to produce bold, award-winning shows with universal appeal and commercial potential.

Since launching in 2018 the company has been awarded an Olivier, three Scotsman Fringe First's and produced seven world premieres across London, New York, nationally on tour and at the Edinburgh Festival. FMP's production of Richard Gadd's *Baby Reindeer* was the Bush Theatre's fastest selling show in history and was due to transfer to the West End in 2020.

In 2020 FMP conceived and produced SHEDINBURGH FRINGE FESTIVAL an online live-streamed festival of theatre, comedy and music in lieu of the Edinburgh Fringe, selling over 4500 tickets and raising over £30,000 towards a fund to support the next generation of artists to make it to the Fringe. SHEDINBURGH returned in 2021.

FMP is led by Francesca Moody MBE who is best known as the original producer of the multi-award-winning *Fleabag* by Phoebe Waller-Bridge, which she has produced globally on behalf on DryWrite, most recently in London's West End at the Wyndham's Theatre, when it was also recorded and broadcast by NT Live, playing in cinemas throughout the world. In 2020 Francesca led and coordinated the Fleabag for Charity campaign and later the Theatre Community Fund with Phoebe Waller-Bridge and Olivia Colman, raising over £2million to support theatrical artists and professionals whose livelihoods and creative futures have been threatened in the wake of Covid-19.

FRANCESCA MOODY PRODUCTIONS

Executive Producer	**Francesca Moody**
Producer	**Harriet Bolwell**
Finance Manager	**Charlotte Lines**

Twitter: @FMP_Theatre
Instagram: @francesca_moody_productions
Facebook: facebook.com/FMoodyProductions
Email: hello@francescamoody.com
www.francescamoody.com

FEELING AFRAID AS IF SOMETHING TERRIBLE IS GOING TO HAPPEN

Marcelo Dos Santos

Acknowledgements

Thanks to Gabby Vautier, Emma Cameron, Emily Hamilton,
Zbigniew Kotkiewicz, Jane Fallowfield, the Royal Court and
Arts Council England for their support on the initial workshop;
Simon Blakey and Sean Butler at The Agency; Maddie Hindes,
Sarah Liisa Wilkinson, Deborah Halsey, Matt Applewhite,
Tamara von Werthern, Jon Barton, Robin Booth, Ian Higham,
Tim Digby-Bell, Kiana Wu, Nick Hern at Nick Hern Books;
Kenny Emson, Jamie Hakim and Patrick Welch for the chats.

M.D.S.

To Rhys Warrington,
for changing everything

4

This text went to press before the end of rehearsals and so may differ slightly from the play as performed.

A MAN *stands with a microphone, in front of a microphone stand he doesn't use, with a stool and a pint of water.*

I'm thirty-six, which is fine.
It's fine.
Is it? I mean it's technically allowed, so.
I'm thirty-six and up until very recently, I'd never been in a proper relationship.
Which is also fine because I have absolutely no fear of dying alone.
Because I'm a very chilled, in-the-moment, sexually adventurous sort of human person.
For example a gentleman once asked if he could eat sushi off me and seeing as it was a Tuesday and life has no meaning I said: 'yeah'.
You know how you do: like, 'yeah'.
Lower-case, super-cool; 'yeah'.
Like you're so tired at the thought of being a human sushi platter AGAIN that you can't even bring yourself to capitalise the y.
What was a little cheeky was that he told me to bring my own sushi.
He offered to pay me back though so romance not entirely dead.
It might have died later though when it turned out the supermarket sashimi had curdled on the bus ride over.

Beat.

Sorry.

Beat.

I'll start again.

I'm thirty-six, and I'm a comedian, although I prefer the title 'sad for pay'.
Or 'professional neurotic'.

.

Or 'a bit like, oh you know what's-his-name with the hair, but
not as funny'.

Sorry.

I'm thirty-six, I'm a comedian and I'm about to kill my
boyfriend.

/

He has excellent teeth; very white with a well-judged gum-to-
tooth ratio.
He wears long-sleeved, light-blue Oxford shirts and baseball
caps, which he is able to take off whenever he wants because
his hair is MAGIC.
He's American which explains the cap, the teeth and the fact he
didn't immediately smash his phone when we matched.
I've discovered over the years that my accent has currency with
Americans, and my man-boy physique holds a strange allure to
the formerly fat.
When I first saw him I sent up a silent prayer.
Dear God, please let it be that he used to eat his feelings as a kid,
was relentlessly bullied and his parents own a beach house in the
Hamptons where we will be wed, amen.

Sorry.
Was the first word I said to him.
Why? He said sounding all American, like they do on the telly.
I don't know but always good to get it in first.
He smiled.
His smile of course, is devastating.
I am devastated.
What's wrong?
Nothing I said. Or is there? Has someone had an accident? Is
there an emergency? Do you need to go? Or shall I go, leave you
to it? Yeah let's do that. Let me pay for your drink and I'll go.
You're funny? he said, and I chose to think the rising of his
voice at the end of the sentence? was his accent rather than
a question.

We're sat on wobbly chairs on the pavement outside a Hackney
Downs pub drinking gin and tonics.

It's early summer; those two first hot days where everyone flashes
their ankles and pretends they live somewhere actually nice.
There are maybe a hundred people strolling the streets, looking
lovely and tan, successfully ignoring the fact we're all going
to die.
Probably quite soon.
It's always amazing to me that.
Why is no one freaking out more?
Why aren't we already in the bunker?
Why am I the only one in a constant state of panic?
Why are we just doing this? This.
Why aren't we running around screaming?
Why do I have to do all the screaming?
I mean I don't but inside I do.
Inside it is... deafening.

He's looking at me.
Sorry, I have resting sad face, but I'm having a lovely time.
He smiled.
That smile.

We get down to business.
This is, after all, an interview.
We state our biographies at each other with the wry detachment
specific to gay men and forensic pathologists.
Distant dad, anxious mothers, dead bodies, blah blah blah.

He's from Boston, Massachusetts.

Beat.

He's from Sacramento, California, yes!, Sacramento,
California: the whole city just one giant tree-lined street.

Total suburbia, close to San Francisco though, he says.

Cool, I say.

Too cool for me, at least when I was young. Too weird as well.
I was a nerdy kid. Now it's too expensive. Like insanely
expensive.

He studied at Reed in Portland, Oregon.

Cool.

Actually quite problematic, quite divided in terms of race and income inequality but you know, coffee.

Ha! Just that, one, HA, like a lunatic, but he's funny, he's funny!

Now I'm doing a PhD.

Cool.

In US prison reform and when he goes back to the States I'll go with him, sod it.
Or can we have a place here *and* in New York?
Or San Francisco?
Preference for New York.
I'll have to move fast though before he realises.
Before he works out.
Shit, he's finished talking.

Cool. (I keep saying cool.)

Well not if you are the prisoner with HIV, no.

Of course, no, not cool for them at all. (I mean…)

Actually for a lot of people prison is the only place they're going to get healthcare including HIV medication, so…

I don't know what to say to that so I say:

Sooo.

But yeah that's me, that's why I'm over here living the London life.

'London life' isn't a thing but he doesn't know that so I smile, making sure not to reveal my teeth.
Gum recession, gaps, tea stains.

What about you?

Oh I've been here ten years now. Northern but not northern-northern you know? (He doesn't.) Not northern enough for actual northerners, not cool enough for London.

I love your accent.

'Cheers,' I say. (We're all posh to them.)

What else?

Oh you know, lonely childhood, anxious mother, dead dad blah blah blah.

And what do you do?

Lots of ways to play this, none of them guaranteed to work.

Believe it or not, I'm a comedian. Ta-dah.

It's only later, when I know him better, when I'm able to read him better, when I'm able to decipher what's an American pause and what's a silence that I realise this was a silence...

But tell me about you, tell me about the bod.

He looks confused.

The bod, the body, the muscles I can see through your shirt, Mr Muscle, Mr Gym-Going-Man you.

I may or may not have poked his chest and I'm aware of an accusatory edge to my voice but he really enjoys talking about his regime of high-intensity interval training so we do that for exactly... forty-seven minutes.

It's just about exercise, diet, exercise, diet. I mean it always is. You just have to be really in it.

I think about saying I want to be under it but resist.

Sorry, it's boring.

No, not at all.

I used to be fat, he reveals. Like really fat. And really bullied.

I thank God, thank you God and sigh.
And the evening seems to sigh around us.
The waitress finds us adorable.
Or him adorable.
He tips heavily, inappropriately, so perhaps not to be totally trusted but still, cute.
And then we're talking about bad dates.

We trade the usual stories of bad breath and catfishing and
there's a frisson to that because that means this.
This is different.
This is a *good* date.

Now the kiss.
Actually no.
Not yet.
The way he licks his lips and teeth before the kiss, like
a toothpaste commercial.
And he does taste delicious.
Fresh but acid from the gin and tonic.
I would very much like to see his penis.
Which I suspect he knows.
That smile again.

Do you want to go see that exhibition next week then?
Presumably we talked about an exhibition.
I have no memory because at one point in the evening he
accidentally-on-purpose lifted up his shirt to reveal what I think
the kids call: semen gutters… and I lost consciousness.

Yes, I'd love that I say and go for another kiss/lunge.
He kindly reciprocates but delicately so as not to wound peels
himself away.
There will be no fucking tonight.
Which is fine.
Which is good.
Which is what we want.
Which is what will make this one different.
Special.
Or I'll never see him again.

On the way home, I buy a giant Haribo bag from the local shop
and as I eat each sweet, I think exercise, diet, exercise, diet.

On the bus Mum rings.
I shouldn't take it because I'm not in the mood but I do.

Well, she says, I'm alright.
I say really?, she says no.
I say oh.

She's lonely; I have no idea what it's like to be a single woman
her age.

I open up 'The App' as she talks.
Very much the usual faces, torsos, sunsets.
I won't name The App because I'm classy but essentially, it's
a dating app which encourages sexual connections and mental-
health issues.
Mum is talking about Grandma.
I send an ass pic to a surly jock.
Mum is worried about the elections.
I agree to pound a twink's 'boy pussy' whatever that actually is,
and then he goes quiet.
I better go I say.
I better go she echoes and then doesn't.
I better go I repeat
Neither of us goes but neither of us is really there.
Are you okay, she asks?
I say of course.
I message Mike and asks if he wants a shag.

And he writes back:

'yeah'

/

Anyone ever cum blood while having sex and feel like you're
going to die?
No one?
Me neither.

/

Mike. Mike? Michael. Michael lives in Hampstead which
involves a walk.
This is firmly in the immediate radius of The App so there's
this substrata of sex data attached to every street.

Grafton Road: fit guy who works in music, surfaces Sunday
morning every week, human equivalent of a hungover wank,
lots of fun actually.

Regis Road: pretty blond bottom very into jockstraps, massive
Tory, lobbied for Esso (not particularly proud of that one).
Courthorpe Road: civil servant from the Treasury who
convinced me to have sex with his boyfriend who was also
secretly on The App.
Again, not my finest hour.

And Pilgrim's Lane: Michael.

Michael is a handsome doctor with a lovely, high, bobbing bum
who is outrageously not my husband.
We're the same age, same height, same half-smile.
Same star sign too – Scorpio – but crucially neither of us *feel*
like Scorpios.
Our dicks look exactly the same, same size, same slight kink to
the left.
I look down and lose track of where he starts and I begin.
He's also a DOCTOR, so... you know: buy a hat.

The problem is the only text he responds to is the 'what's up?'
text
'What's up?'
Like we're high-school jocks rather than thirty-somethings with
weak chins and suspect bowels.
But he can get away with it. He can get away with anything.

I tell him all about the date with the American.
He kisses me passionately, deeply and then asks if I want coke.

I don't want it.
I know I don't want it but I say yes.
So he pulls out a bag of coke from his side table and I see a
copy of the really quite obscure and clever book I'm currently
reading.
I think about us being adorable and comparing notes on the
unreliable first-person narrator. Instead we talk about all the
guys he's shagged in a four-mile radius.
Quite a few we have in common, which is nice.
And it's good.
It's good we can talk about sex.
It's good we can be so open.

It's queer.
It's political.
It's liberating – and the feeling, the feeling what is the feeling?
The edge, the sense of creeping something cold is just the, just
the, ju-ju-ju-ju-ju
just the coke, he says when we try and have sex again and can't.
It's three a.m.

We stare at the ceiling in silence, not touching and he turns and
looks at me.
We shouldn't have done the coke.
I laugh and he laughs back.

Do you like boxing?
I've never watched it.
I've got really into it for some reason, he says. It's very theatrical.
Which is not an enticement, but I say okay.

His arm keeps cramping so he can't hold me and he doesn't like
my arm under his neck but we lie side by side, one whole side
of our bodies touching and I start to find myself getting into the
boxing, enjoying the satisfying simplicity of a contest where
both sides know the rules and each knows what the other wants.

Beat.

And then five, four, three, two, one.

Do you mind going home? I've got an early start.

He's that guy.

/

Anyone ever cum blood while having sex and feel like you're
going to die?
No one?
Me neither.

/

Now, it could be that he's American, the American.
That's what I think at first.
The way his eyes don't register sometimes.

The way they sort of glaze over when I'm being hilarious.
He's very American in that way.
But he's kind.
He cares.
He knows words.
You know, clever ugly left-wing words.
Hegemony.
Neoliberalism
Austerity.
But he also says things like:
Self-love.
Self-care.
Self-actualisation.
I stop myself saying 'the only self I'm interested in is self-abuse'
with a little Mae West shrug of the shoulders.
I stop myself because when I say things like that he goes silent
and his brown eyes go heavy.
It's date two.
Second dates, or recalls as I call them, are tricky.
If I've somehow aced the first date it usually falls apart on
the second.
And if it doesn't I make sure it does.
I'm that guy.

Let's find all the pretty boys in the National Portrait Gallery,
because let's face it, that's the only way to make it bearable,
I say.
(It's a fun game, you should try it.)
I find one I'm very into: Henry Peter Brougham, first Baron
Brougham and Vaux, circa 1778.
Clearly a dirty Tory but just enormous big-dick energy.
Tories by the way are my weakness.
I may never have kissed one but I have eaten cum out of their
jockstraps.
A young Alfred Lord Tennyson would get it.
Sir John William Alcock (ooh-er missus) rocking a World War
One air force uniform
Heroic and naughty.
The American stops at a Henry Lamb self-portrait.
Handsome, I say.

The American doesn't say anything.

Isn't he?

Not as handsome as you, he says.

And it's a line.

It's got to be a line but he doesn't make it a joke, or laugh it off.

He just looks at me with those John Singer Sargent eyes of his

and I find myself going – .

And this is true –

A little weak at the knees.

So shall we do this again?, he asks.

Yes, a thousand times yes.

/

I realise I haven't been on The App forever.

Like literally four days.

Five days.

Maybe even a whole week.

This is something of a record so I'm feeling good about myself.

I boldly greet an astonishing torso I wouldn't normally even

attempt.

For the uninitiated, if you don't want to show your face on

The App, probably because you're over thirty, cheating or

closeted, you can put up a picture of your torso, or and this is

quite popular, a sunset.

Never a sunrise, read into that what you will.

(You should read into it: death.)

The astonishing torso sends a picture of his face, it's grainy but

enough to establish that he has one and a rather fetching dick pic.

Together the images suggest a human male form which seems

to be enough for me at that moment.

I send my location.

'Cool. I can come on my run. Haven't got long though.'

He's oral only.

Ironic really as he says NOTHING.

He has a boyfriend, I assume.

Or he wants me to assume.

He could have a girlfriend, he could be single, he could be

married to a woman and have two children, he could be my

soulmate, he could be the one, but not today.

The speed of the encounter, the silence, the ambiguity is what's
hot/depressing/hot.
Plus he does actually arrive in his running gear, looks to be
about twenty-four, and has a tremendous penis, just terrific,
first rate.
Would recommend.

(It's only a matter of time before The App has a star-rating
option. Just you wait.)

He doesn't want to kiss, of course.
And actually that feels okay.
He lies back on the bed.
I go to work.
He cums.
I don't.
He leaves.
I don't feel shame.
I try not to feel shame.
Because this is what I wanted.
Because I am a very chilled, in-the-moment, sexually
adventurous sort of human person.

/

Three dates.
Four dates.
Five dates.
Five dates with the American and we still haven't had sex.
I feel like alerting *The Guinness Book of Records* but they
presumably have their hands full contemplating the
meaninglessness of their existence.
I mean has anyone ever read that book?

Beat.

Sorry, I thought that might go somewhere but it didn't.

Beat.

Five dates which is two more than is normal.
Or sane.
That's what Gavin says.

Gavin is an extremely handsome comedian which shouldn't be allowed but it gets him on the telly, a lot.

What exactly is the hurt that you are trying to overcome in your comedy, Gavin? That your razor-sharp cheekbones get snagged in turtlenecks?

Fuck off.

(The backstage repartee at The Bearcat in Twickenham is sparkling.)

I think it's a little excessive says Djosephine, but she genuinely moved in with her girlfriend Ziggy after two dates.

That's not a joke, it's true, although it's also a joke because she does a whole set on it.

I think, you are terrible cynics and it means he's interested. Like actually interested in me as a person.

Why? You're dreadful?

No one likes you.

You have SDE.

They call them STIs now.

No, SDE – small-dick energy.

Has he been to see your show yet?

No.

Good.

That was a terrible set.

You're not funny.

What even is a *Guinness Book of Records*?

Et cetera.

/

Date six.

I've shaved my pubes to the bone, because every little helps.

And I've douched, just in case.

We haven't discussed who likes what where yet so I have to be prepared for all eventualities.

I don't really have a preference any more; at this point my sexuality would be best described as passive-aggressive.

Are we going to have sex? I demand over yet another really fun dinner.

(I've only eaten a salad so I'm hanging on by a thread.)

Oh right, he says, which could mean ANYTHING.
I like to take things slow, he says which is... nice?
I guess my face does something because he asks:
Is sex like a big thing for you?
No, not at all. At all.
Then what's the rush?
I don't know.
Is that an English thing?
What?
Saying I don't know when you do.
I don't know. I mean. Yes. Or no. I don't know.
What's going on?

Beat.

What if it's bad?
What if he's repelled by my body?
Because the thing is I can handle rejection, honestly.
I'm used to rejection.
It's actually my safe space but as a rule I prefer to get the
rejection over with quickly so I can get back to my healthy diet
of *Golden Girls* reruns, hate-stalking famous people I used to
know and masturbating to Czech twinks being pissed on.

Beat.

What if we're completely incompatible? What if you take one
look at me naked and?
Why do you always assume the worst?
I don't!
I mean you absolutely do. Remember your eye thing?
And it takes me a minute.
The brain tumour?
Oh yeah it wasn't a brain tumour.
Because nine times out of ten it's all in your head he says.
As if my head weren't the place I live in.
I look at his chin and I wonder if it's a bit too big actually, too
square, like a parody, like someone had drawn it. He's too...
perfect.
Are you okay? he asks.

Totally, sorry was I being boring?
No, you just look sad.
That's impossible, I'm having a brilliant time.
It doesn't have to be jokes the whole time, you know?
Talking of which, do you want to come and see my show on
Friday? I'm playing in Bethnal Green which isn't far from you.
The American nods.
He doesn't smile.
He nods.
Serious.
'That'll take the shine off his bliss,' I think.
That's Beckett.
That's not me.
None of this is me.

/

Dad wanted his wake at the Wetherspoons.
Presumably he wanted to die as he lived.
Sad and a little bit racist.

/

The American turns up on his own.
I told him not to.
I said bring a friend.
Implied in that was bring me into your circle of friends and let's
all hang out, let's all go to cool parties together or Mexican
bars, people go to Mexican bars right? I've seen them, dreadful
people at dreadful Mexican bars let's all go to dreadful Mexican
bars, eat fajitas and be dreadful, let's have a massive wedding
where we invite all our dreadful friends and one of my dreadful
friends gets together with one of your dreadful friends and it's
really funny but they actually seem to like each other, and soon
we're having regular dinner parties together and maybe they get
married and have a baby and name it after one of us because
they met at our wedding, you actually because you have a better
name, but we both get to be honorary guncles and that's quite
nice isn't it? That's actually quite special or maybe we want our
own? Oh my God are we having a baby? But what would be the
best way, surrogacy or adoption? And would we be good

parents? You'd be good obviously, you'd be great, which would hopefully make up for me, minimise the damage but at least we'd have someone to look after us at the end, not that that's a guarantee, not that the future is compatible with the past on that front, not that we can look back any more to understand the future, the future is the science fiction I read as a kid and stopped reading as an adult because it wasn't grown up but they knew didn't they? They saw the fracturing, they saw the cyborgs and the disasters, the plagues and the floods, how can we bring children into that future? How dare we? Besides my child won't like me, as if my child would be at my deathbed as if we won't die alone, as if we don't die all alone anyway.

But funnily enough he didn't seem to pick up on any of that.

He turned up on his own.

He sat not quite in the front row but basically the front row.

Bolt upright – he has excellent posture.

In the half-light, I can see his white teeth.

They're almost ultraviolet.

He's smiling.

He is absolutely smiling.

And he is clapping.

He's a clapper.

Who knew?

He knows when to clap.

He leads the clapping.

The way the laughter seems to crest like a wave into a clap.

He feels the exact point of the crest and he claps or yes.

Yes.

Slaps his thighs.

He slaps his thigh like an eighteenth-century fop highly appreciative of my abundant wit but he does not laugh.

The fucker doesn't laugh.

And I'm being quite funny.

I won't do it now because you know, pressure, but I had them.

I had them.

I felt it and they felt it.

Which doesn't always happen.

I mean it doesn't normally, not for a whole set.

Anyone ever cum blood while having sex and feel like you're
going to die?
No one?
Me neither.

It's a tricky opening line.
But it's a litmus test.
If I'm relaxed, if I get the rhythm right and the audience laughs
we're going to have a good night.
Anyone ever? – sing-song, familiar
Cum blood while having sex? – still light, don't go dark even
though it's dark.
Allow a fraction of a beat for the surprise to land.
And feel like you're going to die? – again light, as surprised
as us.
No one? – genuinely curious.
Me neither – in on the joke.
Laugh.

A call-and-response.

I make my voice do this.
Laugh.
I combine an expected word with an unexpected one.
Laugh.
I say things in threes.
Laugh laugh laugh.
The inappropriate phallic vol-au-vents at my dad's funeral –
surely it feels like we're overcompensating?
The time the guy ate sushi off me – note the alliteration, sweaty,
slippy, sashimi.
My mum watching a film called *Snakes on a Plane* and being
shocked by the snakes.
Each line spontaneous.
Each line landing exactly as planned.
Each line a line leading to another line.
And finally a satisfying reveal at the end.
Catharsis, ejaculation, laughter.

It's like being a musician, composer, and conductor.

Or is it like being a butcher?
There is something cold and mechanical to it.
If I chop here.
If I fillet there the flesh comes apart from the bone just so.
It's easy.
Like everything is easy when you know how.
Like driving.
But people don't applaud you for driving.
People don't love you for your three-point turn.
Or tattoo your face on their bum for a nifty reverse park.
I guess it's the love that's the difference.
But then drivers don't need the applause.
A butcher is quite relaxed, I assume about what the lamb thinks
of him.
Just as well.

But I care, of course, I do.
I'm a comedian.
I'm very obvious, entirely transparent.
I need my audience to laugh.
(hint)
But, and I think this is where I really am special, I very much
resent them when they do.

Their smiles look like rictus grins.
I see the skulls behind the faces bulging.
I bring down the cleaver.
You've been a lovely audience.
If I was capable of love I'd love you all.
Laugh.
Applause.
And he does, he applauds along, he may even have whistled
because he's American but he doesn't laugh.
He hasn't laughed once.

Everyone had a good set.
Everyone's feeling 'buzzed'.
Gavin had some telly people in.
The telly people saw me.
The telly people want to meet me.

You won't be able to open with the cum gag, Gavin says.
'That's what she said' which doesn't make much sense but the
telly people laugh.

The American spends a lot of time talking to Djosephine and
Ziggy.
He's not laughing at them but Ziggy is a comedy groupie so
she's about as funny as that sounds so nothing to worry about
there.
You were funny tonight, Gavin says. And then looking at the
American: 'You bring nothing to the relationship.'
It's objectively a good night.

What's wrong?
I'm so depressed I have only just registered the fact that we're
in his flat.
I've made it into the inner sanctum.
He lives in Hackney with a girl who is watching Netflix in the
living room so we have to go into his bedroom.
I'm in his bedroom.
There is his bed.

What's wrong?
Nothing, I lie.
It was great. I had a great night. Your friends are great.
They're not my friends.
I mean the other comics.
I mean they are my friends we just don't like each other also we
call them comedians. (I'm being a dick.) So...?
So...
What did you think?
You were hilarious.
Okay.
I don't know how you do it.
Do what?
Get up there.
I use my legs.
I mean I didn't get all the references but you know. Amazing.
Amazing.
He kisses me.

I hesitate.

What?

Nothing.

We kiss again.

Can I ask about the bloody cum?

Which is a fair enough question.

Doesn't happen any more, not a big deal, only lasted for three or four... months.

Wow. That must have been.

It's fine. It's all good copy.

Okay.

And he kisses me again but there's still the niggle. Why didn't the fucker laugh?

I didn't think the stuff about my dad really landed. (This is a lie, I'm just fishing, the stuff about my dad was gold.)

He looks at me.

Well it is sad.

Not really.

I mean you were making it into a joke but it was still kinda sad. You were so young.

I was twenty-one.

It was a trauma. Losing your dad at such a pivotal moment in your development, just when you're supposed to be coming into yourself you have to move home and look after your mum? That is a trauma.

It was just a bit about oversized party sausages.

He shrugs: it just makes me sad to think about you being so alone.

That's what he says, just like that, like it's an easy thing to say:

'It just makes me sad to think about you being so alone.'

I have a feeling I've done something terribly wrong but I can't remember what.

I have a feeling I've been caught out in a massive lie.

I have a feeling any second now, someone is going to knock on the door and take me away.

Except.

Except that of course that's what I want him to feel.

I want him to feel sad for me.

I want him to sense the pain beneath the jokes, the dead bodies buried in a shallow grave of weird sex and passive-aggressive asides.

And I want you to sense it too, obviously.

But I don't want to talk about it.

If I wanted to talk about it I wouldn't layer it in irony, encase it in the meta, I wouldn't be making jokes now would I?

But you get that. We get that. We don't have to talk about it?

That would be boring; that wouldn't be funny.

But here, here he is talking about it.

Naming it.

Here he is and yes I'm going to say it.

Seeing me.

And I cry.

Okay.

Happy?

But honestly these are weird tears.

Very weird tears.

They come without trying.

(Without a conscious, constipated attempt to feel something. Without even the aid of Bette Midler in *Beaches*.)

They're just there.

He kisses them which just makes me cry more.

And then I'm laughing like one of those people.

One of those people on the telly feeling things.

Stay here, he says. Stay with me.

And we're kissing and yes.

We're doing the sex but I manage to stay there.

I stay looking into his eyes as we remove each other's clothes.

I mean I do sneak the odd look, presumably he doesn't just want me to look into his eyes the whole –

He holds my face clamped in his hands fixed on his eyes.

(It was mental really but I went with it.)

And actually, actually, when it was just him and me.

When I wasn't distracted.

When I wasn't thinking.

I felt... things... which was...

Nice.
The sex was nice.

Now nice of course is a loaded word.
And I don't mean to say that it was boring.
I just mean I didn't feel shit after.
Which in that moment, I realised may have been a first.
Which makes me cry.
Again.
And he is adorable.
He holds me in the arms and yes, I can't help but notice the arms are the arms of a Disney prince.
And he whispers things, I forget what now and they were probably cheesy but he wasn't afraid to say them.
If it was me in that situation I would already be offering tea and asking if he wanted to be on his own.
Because I'm awful. I'm the worst.
You're beautiful he says.
And I say what's wrong with you?
What do you mean?
You're just perfect? You're perfect aren't you? What's wrong with you?

I've stopped crying by now, just you know, for context and he's moved away.
He's standing in the middle of the room naked.
I don't know how people do that.
Just stand there naked in front of someone else but he does it.
He stands there, naked, looking to all intents and purposes like the guy Michelangelo dumped David for when he got rich and famous and he says – I have to tell you something.
Which of course we know is the end.
Perhaps not the end-end but the beginning of the end.
A state of calm descends on me.
I'm completely serene.
I'm swimming in Lake Me.
It's more like a pond and I've clearly pissed in it but it's mine.
Here it comes.

I can't laugh.

What?

I can't laugh. If I laugh I could die.

What do you mean?

It's a nerve condition.

Are you serious?

Deadly. He says, and almost but doesn't actually laugh.

He can't.

/

Ever hear the one about the comedian with the boyfriend who can't laugh?

/

And it's true.
It is true.
It is a genuine medical condition.
Cataplexy.
It's a bit like narcolepsy which I've always had a fondness for ever since *My Own Private Idaho*.
River Phoenix repeatedly swooning in Keanu Reeves' arms was actually something of a sexual awakening for me.
Is it like that?
He hadn't seen it, of course.
So...
So... If you laugh your head falls off?
Not exactly he says. But worst-case I could die.
Right.
Or there is a risk of permanent paralysis.
Right.
I just have to be careful.
Right.
I've sort of learnt to train myself to be on guard.
Right.
I can feel it coming, he says.
Now?
No. Not now.
I'm using humour to defuse the tension.

I know.
And that's bad?
No.
I just have to not be too funny.
Which shouldn't be a problem.
Which is funny.
Which is a joke so I laugh and then stop myself.
You can laugh, you're allowed to laugh, it's just me. I can't laugh.
Okay.
Is this going to be a problem? He asks.

/

He's there and then he isn't.
Laughing with those teeth.
A pop of his pretty pink tongue.
White teeth, pink tongue still caught in the blink of my eye.
And then he's gone.

/

Of course it's not a problem.
And, dear readers, wait for it... it isn't.

Imagine almost complete happiness.
No, me either but try.
We start seeing each other repeatedly, regularly in a way that
starts to resemble, gasp,
people in a relationship.
I have no experience of this, I'm just basing it off *Friends*.
(My entire generation does and yes frankly that is a problem but
let's pretend it isn't for a minute okay? Yes? No? Great.)
There are the galleries where suddenly we are in complete
agreement about every painting,
trips to the cinema to see obscure foreign-language films
I finally seem able to enjoy, documentary nights in his bedroom.
Actually he's very into documentaries, the more hard-hitting the
better.
What with the head-falling-off situation we spend a lot of time
snuggling down to the latest doc about the Cambodian killing
fields and smiling.

At each other.

Not the.

I meet a couple of his friends, once.

The flatmate knows my name.

I think she's called Charlotte.

Or Francesca.

One of the two.

Neither of us have ever seen her not watching Netflix in the living room.

The summer is long and endless-feeling.

I get a bike, immediately realise I've forgotten how to ride a bike; turns out it's not at all like riding a bike.

It's actually really hard.

I'm wobbly but strangely fearless as long as I'm with him.

We cycle to Essex which turns out is basically the countryside and quite nice.

The American is an excellent cook so I put on weight but in interesting places.

My body is changing, I'm filling out.

Like someone has drawn my outline in ink, finally.

I'm me but a new me.

A grown-up me.

And that in itself feels exciting.

And the porousness of long summer days into long summer nights and the him and the me grows until there's no need to clarify whether we *are* seeing each other because we *only* see each other.

He doesn't come to my gigs.

I don't need him to.

I mean I don't go to his lectures do I?

The demand for affirmation seems suddenly insane.

What on earth am I doing, talking into people's faces demanding their laughter, demanding their love?

Because it's not love is it?

What I have with the American.

That...

Beat.

I experiment with my material.

Tone down the trauma and the bloody cum.

I start talking about how different but compatible me and the American are.

Stuff about British versus American sensibilities.

He's always the hero, and I'm still the idiot but you know, a more likeable idiot.

More Hugh Grant less Philip Roth.

Djosephine doesn't like the new material but she's in a bad mood.

She recently broke up with her girlfriend, Ziggy.

Apparently Ziggy recited the whole of the Dead Parrot Sketch during sex one night and Djospehine snapped.

Ruined the vibe? I asked.

Ruined the sketch. She has terrible timing.

We agree that's a good line and she should use it.

Gavin's into my new set which may or may not be a worry.

I have a screen test for a new panel show coming up.

Life is good.

I text Michael, the doctor.

Just you know, 'how are you?'

He responds

'What's up?'

And what's up is my penis, immediately just like that.

I take a moment.

I breathe.

(I'm breathing now. The American has got me into something called breath work. Turns out I've been breathing wrong my entire life which I fully believe.)

So, I breathe and say:

'Hey, dude.' (I don't know why we do that.) 'Not much. I'm good though. Got a boyf exclamation mark.'

And then press send.

Immediate relief.

He writes back immediately in flowing prose I didn't know he was capable of about how happy he was for me, how lucky the guy is and on and on and how we should get tea some time.

Tea?

I think about not responding but that would be rude, that would
be game-playing and there's no need to game-play because
we're just friends.
Thanks. Tea would be lovely. Actually. I'm doing a stand-up in
Kilburn tomorrow. Not too far from you question mark. Want to
come question mark.'
He doesn't respond.
Which is fine.
Which is good.

The next night in Kilburn, I look for him in the audience.
There's a feeling.
What is that feeling?
I feel shit about myself that's it.
I channel it into the comedy.
I phase out the American and become comedically, tragically
single again.
I get more laughs.

/

Have you ever stroked a kitten and thought?: 'my hand is bigger
than its head and if I just...'

/

The American and I spend a weekend in the week together.
We go to Highgate Cemetery.

We comment on the weather – so warm.
We comment on the flowers – pretty.
We've started to do that ever since we got matching flower
boxes from the overpriced garden centre in De Beauvoir.
His are doing very well.
Mine are hanging on in there but I'm worried about the
chrysanthemums.

This is boring, I think.
We're being boring, I'm being boring.
Except, except even though we have said nothing interesting,
nothing original, nothing funny we still appear to like each other.
Which is new.
Which is even a bit hot.

I look at him properly.

The dappled light makes him seem to flicker.

Like he's made up of small dots, which make sense from afar but disappear when you get close.

/

Michael texts about missing the Kilburn show.

Twenty-three days after the Kilburn show.

No worries, I reply instantly. How are you?

Good he texts, and then sends through a picture of a naked guy puckered out on his bed.

'Hahaha. Is this happening live?' I write.

He responds, it is.

I don't respond

I shouldn't respond.

I send a winky face.

He sends one back.

When I find myself wanking to the message exchange later, it's not because of the picture Michael sent but of the almost painfully exquisite eroticism of our two winking emojis.

One on top of the other.

/

The American doesn't get slapstick.

This isn't surprising but I'm acting surprised.

It's absolutely pure comedy, I explain.

I don't find it funny.

That's not possible. It's instinctively funny.

To see someone getting hurt?

No, it's really important they don't get hurt. That's the difference between comedy and tragedy. What's funny, I pontificate, is the complete upturning of reality in one moment. I'm in a pub, I'm drinking a pint, I'm leaning back towards the bar because that's where the bar is but it's not and I fall through.

I don't get it.

I think it's about death.

You think everything is about death.

No, listen. We see someone fall over and get hurt. That's not funny. We see someone lean against a bar but there's no bar

there, he falls through and then gets up that's funny. Something
weird has happened, something out of the ordinary has
happened but no one is hurt.
How is that about death?
One of these days we're going to fall and we're not going to get
up but not this time. In that moment we realise how alive we are
and the relief is the laughter.
It all just seems silly to me.
Okay, what do you find funny?
You know what I find funny.
Holocaust documentaries?
Shut up. You, I find you funny.
Lies.
I find lots of things funny.
Name them.
Like people, comedians?
Or whatever.
Bill Hicks.
Doesn't count.
Why doesn't that count?
Because I love Bill Hicks, everyone loves Bill Hicks but no one
actually laughs out loud at Bill Hicks. What makes you laugh?
Why? Why do you need to know what makes me laugh?
And it's a good question.

/

The therapist looks at me for the first time.
She's not a real therapist.
I can't afford that.
She's a nice girl from the NHS with no detectable shoulders.
What I do and what we can offer is something called CBT,
which stands for Cognitive Behavioural Therapy.
I just need to talk to someone.
Also you do know that in some circles, CBT stands for Cock
and Ball Torture?
(She shifts in her seat.)

Thank you for filling in the questionnaires.
No problem.

I can see for the section where we ask you to grade on a scale a feeling that something terrible is going to happen you have put ten out of the maximum ten?

Yes.

And for the question about whether you might be at risk of hurting others, you've put ten out of ten, written YES and underlined it three times.

Yes, that's what I wanted to talk about.

Can I ask why you've also drawn a smiley face?

Well, I also want you to like me.

(She makes a note in her pad for the first time, which I'm excited about.)

Can you outline the nature of the risk you pose?

Have you ever stroked a kitten and thought 'my hand is bigger than its head and if I just...'

So you want to kill a kitten?

No, I want to make my boyfriend laugh.

(She looks confused.)

Which will kill him. It's a medical thing, if he laughs his head falls off.

My therapist laughs and stops herself.

Actually, I'm doing a show in Putney next week if... No, see this is the problem. I need an audience to laugh. I need you to laugh. I especially need him to laugh.

Why?

I don't know I just do.

Pause.

Maybe because I have feelings for him?

She nods encouragingly.

Would you say you have negative thought patterns?

I would say so, yes.

Do you have a tendency to catastrophise?

Every second of every day but that's not the point. What I want to know is am I a psychopath?

So what I do and what we can offer is something called CBT, which stands for Cognitive Behavioural Therapy.

Sorry.
Sorry.
I'll try again.

Ever since I texted Michael.
Ever since I invited him to the gig.
Ever since then things have been different.

I start feeling self-conscious around the American.
The calm, the intellectual nights out, even the nice sex.
The calm, perfect sex feels like a test.

I'm struggling to have normal conversations, instead I do bits at
him, into his face.
I turn everything into a routine.
I catch myself sometimes and I say sorry, sorry.
Stop saying sorry, it's fine.
I think about tickling him.
His mouth fully open and the laugh.
The laugh?
What would that sound like?
I think out of the buff American would come the cutest little
giggle.
And he is a bit camp, which I love.
I love him, I think.
He's so fucking nice I want his head to fall off.

And the thing is, no one would be able to prove anything – he
has a condition.
It's the perfect crime.
But I'd confess.
I'd have to.
The hardest thing wouldn't be jail.
It would be facing his family.
And mine.
My mum's face as the jury says guilty.
Because I am.

Shall we watch *Nazi Megastructures* on Netflix?
Perfect I say.
And breathe shallowly.

I'm losing weight again.
Losing definition.

/

The twink lives in the flats next to Arsenal Stadium.
The view from his window is a series of concrete squares and
a suspended triangle of bright-green pitch.

Do you like football I ask?

What he says?

Football?

Well I like their jockstraps he says and pulls down his shorts to
reveal a porcelain-smooth ass in a black jockstrap.

We're in his room.
I can hear his flatmates, a square straight couple making a stir fry.

He pulls out a mysterious powder from his bedside table.

What is it?

And he shrugs in a way that makes us both laugh although I have
no idea why.
And then he taps the packet.
Do I want some?

I shouldn't because I've got to be up early.
I shouldn't because I've got *that* audition for the panel show
tomorrow.
I shouldn't for a number of reasons I don't think about.
I shrug back.

I appear to be inside the twink, which is nice.
Nice in a warm-bath sort of way.
I look at him more closely.
He doesn't make any noise.
His face is totally unreadable.
I'm inside him but I have no idea what he's thinking.
I pull out and just like that he changes positions like this has
been agreed, like it's choreographed but I have no idea when we
were taught it and who taught it to us.

He grinds up on me in a way that hurts slightly.
He moans.
Is that good? Am I turning you on? I ask.
Yeah baby.
I'm fairly certain I'm older than him.
I can hear his flatmates watching TV next door.
I try and work out what they're watching.

Antiques Roadshow.

/

The audition is the next day, and strangely enough does not go
well.
They went in a different direction.
They actually said that.
The American takes me out for dinner to commiserate.
I get drunk.
Fuck 'em. Just fuck 'em. I hate TV anyway et cetera.
It's a terrible life I tell him.
You make it sound like you don't have a choice.
I don't.
Of course you do. What else do you want to do?
Anything else I say. Literally anything but I can't.
Okay. What though? You must have wanted to do something
else when you were a kid.
I wanted to be prime minister.
Oh God.
I know. Crisis averted.
Kinda.
Do you ever feel like you've never actually made a choice, you
just did stuff and then stuff happened and then somehow this is it.
This is your life? Like how did that happen?
But your life's not all bad is it?
And I know what I'm supposed to say – and I say it.
No it's not all bad.
I give him a loving look.
I project warmth.
I consciously project warmth.
I may or may not be a psychopath.

What's wrong?
Nothing.
You look stressed.
I'm not stressed.
Just breathe.
Oh God don't make me do the breathing.
You like the breathing.
I did but I don't any more. I'd quite happily stop breathing
forever right now.
Don't say that.
I'm joking.
It's not funny.
Everyone's a critic today.
I'm sorry, I'm just annoyed I fucked up the audition.
Did you try?
What do you mean?
Sudden stab of suspicion.
Did you try your best? All you can do is try your best.
Silence.

/

Michael texts again.
I don't respond though.
I don't respond.
I don't think.

A drug dealer on the way to Michael's asks if I want coke and
I say yes, which comes as a surprise but appears to be true.
I mean it's going to be *awful*.

You can see Hampstead Heath from Michael's living room.

You're getting skinny he says.

He shifts so we're facing each other: You look good skinny.
Healthy skinny.

I look away.

He moves his knee so it touches mine.

I stay very still but I don't move away.

Have you heard of cataplexy?

No, well, sort of. Is that the laughing thing? Is that the latest thing you've got?

Stop making me out to be a hypochondriac.

You are a hypochondriac.

Yes but that doesn't mean I'm not ill. Or won't be. I mean if there's one thing in life that's guaranteed.

Have you ever actually seen anyone die? He asks.

No.

And it's true.
I never saw Dad die.
He died in hospital and I didn't make it in time.
I can't even be sure I saw his body before the funeral.
All I remember is my mum crying.
Crying is not the right word.

Talk to me after you have, he says.

Sorry, I say.

It's fine.

He leans forward for the kiss.

Oh so this is it?
This is a choice.

I kiss Michael.

I feel okay.
I don't feel stressed.
I don't feel guilty.
It's weird how fine I feel.
I actually feel suddenly powerful.
I know how to do this.
I suggest we get another guy around.
Are you sure? Michael asks and I say... yeah why not?

We hang on opposite ends of his bed looking at The App, occasionally showing each other blurry pictures of strangers' cocks and snorting coke.

This one?
He holds up his phone to reveal a guy's face.
Unremarkable, inoffensive, funny lighting but beggars can't be choosers.

Him.

He takes ages to arrive.
The lighting was indeed funny and the picture was old.
He takes off his top self-consciously and asks who wants to get fucked.
We look at each other unsure.
Michael looks away, and even though I don't want to, seeing as it was my idea I say 'me, please'.

His dick is an odd fit and he puts on a voice to say things like: dirty slut, dirty whore, going to fill you up.
I make sure the condom is in place and make noises.
Michael doesn't make eye contact.
I lie back and close my eyes.

I immediately see the American's smiling face exploding against the back of my eyelids.
I open them.
The Random is still going at it.
I look around.
I can't see Michael.
He's gone.
I look back to see the Random has a camera.
Hey! Stop it.
I turn my face away.
Stop filming
You look hot.
Stop it.
I bury my face in the mattress.
Oh well, I think.
He keeps going.
I wait for him to stop.
After a while the Random cums.

I wait until I hear him get dressed.
The tinkle of his belt buckle.
And leave before I move.

Michael is on his sofa.
He gives me a lopsided grin.

I sit beside him.

Did you have fun? He asks.

What do you mean?

I snuggle into him.

He doesn't quite give.

In fact, he pulls away.

And then five four three two one.

Actually do you mind going home? I've got an early start.

And I say... of course, of course, no worries, obviously, cool,
great, wicked (?), and as I'm leaving: cheers. Mate...

I catch him letting out a sigh of relief as the door closes fast
behind me.

I go home.

The American has texted. Of course he has.

I should tell him.

I should tell him everything.

Explain everything. He'd understand.

He always understands everything, before I do, even.

He's so good.

Too good.

The tinkle of the Random's belt buckle.

I text him.

Wait.

I don't text.

I just show up at the American's flat.

Better.

It's midnight.

I don't ask.

I don't text.

I just show up at the American's flat.

Like they do in movies.

Like they do in *Friends* except I can still feel the lube in my hole and actually, actually, it turns out to be quite awkward because he's not in.

Charlotte or Francesca is though and she lets me inside.

She's actually quite nice, we watch Netflix for a bit and then I go into his bedroom.

It's surprisingly messy, the remains of his breakfast by his bed, a cereal bowl, a banana peel.

Something about the spoon in the bowl and the bits of oats stuck to the bowl makes him feel real and I start crying.

I hear his voice outside.

He opens the door.

I stay seated, and cling to the edge of his bed, very aware all of a sudden that I'm still quite high.

Hello you. What's up?

I'm sorry.

Why?

I fucked up.

What happened?

And I tell him.

I tell him about the jogger, the twink.

He doesn't give much away.

I tell him about Michael.

About our texts.

About the threesome no one wanted.

And how I'd had enough.

And how all I really wanted was him.

He stands up.

Zach, I say.

His name is Zach.

Or maybe Dawson, or Chandler? It doesn't really matter.

You are so interesting and clever and you've introduced me to so many great documentaries about the Holocaust.

Don't do that.

Sorry. I'll start again. (*Pause*.) I fuck up. I keep fucking up, but I don't want to, I don't want to any more. I just do it because it's easier. Which makes no sense I know but this feels rare and special but really, really fragile and I'm really scared. I know that's not enough and every bit of me wants to do a bit right now and maybe I am right now, fuck me. But I'm trying, I'm trying not to. I'm trying to say. You know what I'm trying to say.

I don't. I honestly don't.

I'm trying to say...

Well?

What?

Say it then.

What do you mean?

Say the words.

And...

And?

I.

I.

I.

Can't.

Okay, he says and turns away.

(*Quickly*.) I love you.

It's the first time I've said it aloud ever.

I hope it's enough.

It doesn't feel enough.

(*Louder*.) I love you.

(*Softer*.) I love you.

He is very quiet.

Very quiet.

It's not working.

It's supposed to work.

It always works on TV.

(*From the floor.*) I stand up too quickly to reach out to him and
bash my head against a dangling lampshade which wasn't there
a minute ago.
I step back into the cereal bowl, try and steady myself but my
other foot finds the banana peel.
I fall flat on my back.
Splat.

Beat.

I hear a sound I don't recognise at first.
A giggle.
Then a laugh.
A camp-as-tits laugh.
I see him standing above me, laughing with those teeth.
A pop of his pretty pink tongue.
White teeth, pink tongue.
And then he's gone.
And the laughing stops.
I hear a gurgling.
I pull myself up.
I see his legs sticking out from behind the other side of the bed.
I run towards the legs.
His body doesn't seem right.
The angles are strange but his eyes are still open.
I call out his name.
The eyes stop.
His eyes just stop.
And I'm not supposed to say this but there is a little part of me
that is glad.
There is a little part that thinks I could never have made it work.
There is a little part of me that wonders if he was always too
good to be true.
And then I hear his breathing stop and everything in me falls
apart.

He cries.

And then.
And then.

And then just like that…
He winks.
The little fucker smiles… and winks.

Beat.

(*Quietly.*) Thank you. You've been a lovely audience.

Blackout.

End.

A Nick Hern Book

Feeling Afraid as if Something Terrible is Going to Happen first published in Great Britain in 2022 as a paperback original by Nick Hern Books Limited, The Glasshouse, 49a Goldhawk Road, London W12 8QP, in association with Francesca Moody Productions

Feeling Afraid as if Something Terrible is Going to Happen copyright © 2022 Marcelo Dos Santos

Marcelo Dos Santos has asserted his right to be identified as the author of this work

Cover photography by The Other Richard; cover design by Thread

Designed and typeset by Nick Hern Books, London

Printed in Great Britain by Mimeo Ltd, Huntingdon, Cambridgeshire PE29 6XX

A CIP catalogue record for this book is available from the British Library

ISBN 978 1 83904 102 0

CAUTION All rights whatsoever in this play are strictly reserved. Requests to reproduce the text in whole or in part should be addressed to the publisher.

Amateur Performing Rights Applications for performance, including readings and excerpts, by amateurs in English should be addressed to the Performing Rights Manager, Nick Hern Books, The Glasshouse, 49a Goldhawk Road, London W12 8QP, *tel* +44 (0)20 8749 4953, *email* rights@nickhernbooks.co.uk, except as follows:

Australia: ORiGiN Theatrical, Level 1, 213 Clarence Street, Sydney NSW 2000, *tel* +61 (2) 8514 5201, *email* enquiries@originmusic.com.au, *web* www.origintheatrical.com.au

New Zealand: Play Bureau, PO Box 9013, St Clair, Dunedin 9047, *tel* (3) 455 9959, *email* info@playbureau.com

United States of America and Canada: The Agency (London) Ltd, see details below

Professional Performing Rights Applications for performance by professionals in any medium and in any language throughout the world (and amateur and stock performances in the United States of America and Canada) should be addressed to The Agency (London) Ltd, 24 Pottery Lane, Holland Park, London W11 4LZ, *fax* +44 (0)20 7727 9037, *email* info@theagency.co.uk

No performance of any kind may be given unless a licence has been obtained. Applications should be made before rehearsals begin. Publication of this play does not necessarily indicate its availability for amateur performance.

Woodland
CARBON
www.woodlandcarbon.co.uk
NICK HERN BOOKS
Printed on Carbon Captured paper